AF422856

TRAILER

What America went through in its early founding provides an example of a new grounding as a society. That might also be true in your part of the world. This book tries to capture and convey a "rebirth in voice of a people and soul of a nation." Even if America isn't your home country, you might be in a situation of strife like ongoing war, civil disturbances, storm recovery or some other form of 'social or political insecurity'.

The chapters tee-up our approach to this rebirth, through worthwhile results at the right timing. Each chapter features a quote tied to, influenced or inspired by Thomas Paine, the Englishman turned American and 'founding influencer.' The chapters might not have all the answers but bring a message for turnaround and 'turn up', including the Declaration of Emergence.

This book will inform, inspire and invigorate on having a better sense for America's journey. Whether immigrant or native-born, youth or young adult, Gen X, Millennial or Gen Z, it's a fresh look at America over 250+ years. It serves as a primer for career potential, community involvement and social impact. Messages in history, civics and culture are like what a reggae music icon once sang about as "movement of a people", working on something bigger than self.

PUBLIC

GOOD

SENSE

Rebirth in Voice of a People and Soul of a Nation

Douette O. Cunningham

First Edition

© 2026 by Douette O. Cunningham

Public Good Sense: Rebirth in Voice of a People and Soul of a Nation

ISBN:
Paperback: 979-8-90190-405-3
Hardcover: 979-8-90190-406-0

1. History   2. Civics   3. Culture   4. Inspirational   5. Social Impact
6. Self-Development

Bibliography references, reading list included.

Published by:

DOC Communications Publishing
P.O. Box 6223
Somerset NJ 08875

"Purposefully Explicit Content"

ALL RIGHTS RESERVED

Printed in the United States of America.

Dedication

To God for granting me vision in service with cherished memories.

To my wife, daughters and extended family who were there in low moments.

To my village who welcomed and supported me in their midst.

To all who labor for family, career, community, country and a movement.

Table of Contents

Preface: The Task

"The simpler anything is, the less liable it is to be distorted."

It was a cold December morning in New Jersey with bright sunshine and light wind. The forecast was for rain by midday and a rise in temperatures. With another series of blog posts and online blasts finished the previous day, there was some downtime to think about what's next on the writing schedule. Then the 'wonder and imagination' machine got going.

As end of year plans began looking sooner rather than later, there was a feeling of excitement for an upcoming speaking engagement as well as joy for what the holiday season brings. Then it occurred that the new year is not too far off as America gets ready to celebrate its 250th birthday in a few months on July 4th. This is often packaged as parades by day and fireworks by night.

Every year we get to have one day that's ours to do whatever we like. Whether it's a milestone or not, it's a chance to reflect and reset. At the end of the calendar year, the start of a new year or spring season, or a new school year in the fall, each presents a similar self-check. You might certainly expect America's birthday milestone to be an 'annals-of-time check' and a good reason to advance civic spirit considering the gravity of the occasion. This moment of year-end reflection sparked the book project.

The news of the past year had its share of jaw droppers and head scratchers. From stories on a crisis of governing in America leading up to a government shutdown or the tragedy in natural disaster from damage brought by hurricane Melissa to Jamaica and other parts of the Caribbean. In different ways, folks were dealing with confusion, frustration, exhaustion and maybe even desperation.

What might it take to feel a new sense of hope and optimism, under the circumstances? For things to be different, there would have to be an awakening, like a shift in consciousness. In life this is true on a personal level as you begin to have greater spiritual or emotional awareness. In religious circles some say a kind of rebirth occurs in mind and spirit. But in the case of personal dilemma or political drama, the awakening among citizens also involves a rebirth in voice.

This book tries to capture and convey the chance to have a rebirth in voice of a people and soul of a nation. Even if America isn't your home country, you might be in a situation of strife like ongoing war, civil disturbances, storm recovery or some other form of 'social or political insecurity'. The chapters might not have all the answers but will bring a message for turnaround and 'turn up.'

What America went through in its early founding provides an example of how we approach a new grounding as a society. That might also be true in your part of the world. The chapters go from having us tee-up our approach to this rebirth, all the way through seeing worthwhile results at the right timing. Each chapter features a quote tied to, influenced or inspired by Thomas Paine, the Englishman, turned American and 'founding influencer.' Along the way in the book there're also reading "pit-stops to let things breathe" with the 'click note' highlight. As opposed to 'cliff notes', these short boosts could be where some of the aha moments might click.

Paine helped arouse the consciousness of the nation, making the case for the Declaration of Independence and America's founding. The documents and ideals that later came out of that period were next-level stuff in those times. Where we are in the ongoing experiment and evolution, having arrived at America's 250th birthday is no small feat. So, this book makes the case for next-level stuff as a 'Declaration of Emergence' and the next chapter in 'public good sense' for generations to come. Part of that message introduces the social-edge campaign & platform *See America In Color* (SAIC), which was born out of frustration from a series of national news stories.

The chapters are written with an immigrant's eye from trying to know more about America's past, understand the present and rally the future. It includes learning from the journey of those who emigrated, got transported, as well as were native born, and how that influenced their perspective on things. For many years there's been a feeling of awe with some of the retold stories of trial & triumph, including Dr. King's 'I Have a Dream' speech. It eventually became clearer as to why the curiosity. As a Baptist preacher, Dr. King would deliver messages quoting scripture.

This book takes us on a journey, with a message that's delivered with the skill of a 'civics preacher' who's walking in the shoes of history and looking to the future like a prophet. It calls out what was, sounds off on what is and lays out what can be. That's sometimes referred to as forthtelling and foretelling. It takes inspiration as spoken to an Old Testament prophet in Habakkuk 2:2-3 (NIV), Then the Lord replied: "Write down the revelation and make it plain on tablets so that a herald may run with it. For the revelation awaits an appointed time; it speaks of the end and will not prove false. Though it lingers, wait for it; it will certainly come and will not delay." These chapters reveal how my life's journey helped forge writing the vision and making it plain.

Click Note: *The message herein will help to set America free from some of the 'isms and schisms' that seem to stir-up our struggle or hold us back.*

A practical reason for this book is based on my earlier professional experience as a computer engineer. One of the roles back then was being a part of a team that performed root cause analysis on the software system. This would happen after the latest version was delivered to owner/clients in the telephone industry and installed in their communication network. The purpose was to review the millions of lines of software code that made the system work. The idea was to find 'bugs' in the system that caused or could potentially lead to operating errors.

This step in the process was important for quality assurance. What was learned would then be 'fixed' in the next version of the product. Taking that approach as a model, a similar objective was applied in trying to understand the issues of our time. This meant doing a kind 'social analysis' to better understand the root causes of some of the confusion, conflicts and frustration that others expressed. It was also a means to figure out how to minimize or eliminate the 'bugs' that's been causing these issues and to elevate our collective understanding in the next version of America's road to a more perfect Union.

Consider that in the spirit of the Declaration of Independence, Dr. King's 'I Have a Dream' speech, some of the other patriotic moments or social shifts from America's story, the message in these pages will help to set America free from some of the isms and schisms that seem to stir-up our struggle or hold us back. Here's a chance to engage and embrace the idea that public good sense will help set the stage for a new mindset, skillset and jet-set in how we do America and live our best life.

The book is also a kind of love letter to my birth Country of Jamaica and adopted country of the United States of America. No matter where you find yourself reading this, as Dr. Martin Luther King Jr once said, "The time is always right to do what's right." Or as President John F. Kennedy declared, "Ask not what your country can do for you, but what you can do for your country." So, if you find yourself trying to read this book in one swoop, then 'whoop whoop'! This happens all the time when we listen to our favorite artist's release of new music or binge-watch that tv series.

Chapter 1: The Tee-up

"The true foundation of a republic is equal right of every citizen in his person and property and in their management of it."

After the early shots were fired in Lexington and Concord Massachusetts, America was on the road to revolution. This came as a buildup of concern and frustration with various taxes that were levied on the colonies by England's King George III. There was this feeling that something had to change. But what that might look like was up for debate.

Many of the founders were influenced by the Enlightenment Age, and the idea of natural rights. This was the dawning of what later became known as 'inalienable rights' in the Declaration of Independence. Around late 1775, Thomas Paine began writing 'Common Sense', which was first released in early 1776. The book further inspired a sense of new beginnings in the nation as its message of self-governance and self-determination spread across the colonies.

When early settlers first landed on America's shores they came in waves across two regions. The first group landed in Virginia, many looking for new markets to trade their goods. They were often described as being part of the merchant class. They had money on their minds which meant that region became the cradle of enterprise. This strongly influenced their governing philosophy around free trade and property value but also opened the door to slavery.

Emerging from that was the early stages of the Transatlantic slave trade. Africans were gathered and shipped against their will from West Africa to the Caribbean where they'd provide free labor to farm the crops being sent back to England and other parts of Europe. Then America got into the act for its own wealth-building gains. While America's founding as a republic was meant to provide equal right of every citizen in his person, property and the management of it, African Americans got the short-end of the stick by being second-class and seen as three-fifths human.

The other group of early settlers landed in Massachusetts (New England), looking to be new members of a just society, as they fled a sense of religious persecution. They're often described as pilgrims since their journey was a pilgrimage across parts of Europe, coming to North America. Other times they might be described as puritans, because they were looking for a fresh start at religious practice in a 'pure' sense. So, the New England region became the cradle of change.

The distinction between these two main groups of early American settlers is important for understanding how some of the 'culture war' battles played out in history and show up in current times. Sometimes it's a question of who's getting ahead (or feeling left behind) when it comes to the distribution of public funds. Sometimes it's a battle in ideology, whether religious, political or social. Those battles began in the colonies of Massachusetts and Virginia, as well as the hills of Jamaica. The Maroons in Jamaica, were a group of escaped slaves living in those hills, who decided they'd rather survival by a 'destiny of choice' than sellout to slavery.

The rebellions spread to other points particularly along population lines. In the case of America, the battle for Independence was initially one of freedom to set their own agenda without the intrusion of the British Monarchy. That was freedom from economic control and social interference. But not long after in America and Jamaica, there'd be another set of battles around freedom from oppression. This was seen in slave revolts which took on new life as blacks saw that they were not being treated or valued as equals under the sun. In the human experience as it played out in America and the Caribbean, there's been this difference in how freedom is viewed and how it's to be achieved. Furthermore, throughout history these same battles seem to resurface and take on new forms in the hearts & minds of factions in a nation.

Click Note: *While America's founding as a republic was meant to provide equal right of every citizen in his person, property and the management of it, African Americans got the short-end of the stick by being put in second-class status and seen as three-fifths human.*

To advance a new 'founding' or support for the next chapter of a nation's journey or your life's work, it's important to connect the dots across history, civics and culture. This takes learning from past mistakes and shortcomings towards positive social impact, political will and personal change. This means having resources matters not just for the well-connected and well-off but also being well-intentioned for the general welfare and well-being of the nation. This means not just buying-into what you're told by public officials and media personalities, but also tapping-in to who you are in mind, body and core.

There's nothing wrong with having wealth. It's just that when you connect the dots over time in history, you'll see that there've been those who see themselves as part of 'we the people' and others who place themselves above 'we the people'. Some see things more about profit than purpose which might reveal some of the thinking that led to slavery. Others see the value of both profit and purpose, which in business circles is often called the double-bottom line.

That can be true across family, community and country. When you connect the dots over time in ancestry you'll stumble on elements of your family's past that might serve as a springboard for your future. So how we tee-up the next chapter around 'public good sense' is to have history help us to see what came before, civics help us chart what we can become, and culture help us do-it-up in substance and live-it-up in style by making the past, present and future come alive.

Chapter 2: The Test

"These are the times that try men's soul."

As the battles during the Revolution raged on, there were small wins, big losses and near-death moments. These came with times of doubt, especially when finding their backs against the wall. With history as our guide, we see times of losing the battle but eventually winning the war, which wasn't a guarantee. It was during low moments in the struggle that Paine penned the words, "These are the times that try men's souls."

While history shows periods of war-led independence revolution, as a nation we've gone through periods of people-led civic revolution as well. There've been various suffrage movements in abolition, discrimination, women's rights, segregation and more. What came after the dust finally settled on the original American Revolution battlefield was the founding of a new nation that declared its independence with these impactful words:

"We hold these truths to be self-evident that all men are created equal, that they are endowed by their Creator with certain unalienable rights, that among them are life, liberty and the pursuit of happiness."

Those words became the foundation of what would follow in language, leadership and legacy. While they're the most often quoted from that founding document, that's just one part of the script. Otherwise known as the preamble, they are just a warmup to the full text. The Declaration also includes a list of 27 grievances that the colonies laid out as the reason for separation from British rule. This might have been the first place in America's founding documents where the idea of grievances appeared. It was also from this list that the tenets of the Constitution and Bill of Rights started to take shape.

The first grievance said the following, "He has refused his Assent to Laws, the most wholesome and necessary for the public good." That's basically the colonies saying that King George had refused to approve local laws which were most needed for the public good. Clearly, the idea of public good was high on the minds of the founding fathers.

The Declaration then ends with a resolution in these words: "And for the support of this Declaration, with a firm reliance on the protection of divine Providence, we mutually pledge to each other our Lives, our Fortunes and our sacred Honor." In other words, the grievances weren't listed for unsavory or bad conscience reasons. They were outlined to forge a 'new and improved' experience as colonies. Well, that's not where the story ends.

Click Note: *America's new 'founding' needs to have a different incentive and fulfillment structure where folks are celebrated for living out their better angels, not their worst instincts.*

In taking a quick trip through history from that point forward you'll see how various other times have tested men's souls. For about the first 20 years of America's journey, governing happened without political parties. Then by the presidential elections of 1796 two distinct parties emerged: The Federalists and the Democratic-Republicans. John Adams who became America's second President was from the Federalist party. As happened then, the lead-up to elections can sometimes be a time of political crosswinds and uneasiness.

There was a period in Jamaica's history and in other Caribbean and African countries during the initial years of independence where turmoil and tension would arise due to unhappy groups of people. This was often when populist leaders gained attention and traction by making promises of policy reversal and social rejection. This is also why George Washington, in his farewell address after serving two terms as America's first President, warned about 'political factionalism'. In a sense, elections are basically a test of a nation's commitment to democracy.

The rising energy and anger from factions can sometimes carry over into violence and civil unrest. We saw this during the 70s when Jamaica experienced some of the most brutal years in political violence. It was also during that time when Bob Marley gained reggae ambassador status and saw fit to call out the leaders for the country's political turmoil. As the movie 'Bob Marley: One Love' reminded us, he and his band organized a big 'One Love' concert (as the popular song suggests) to serve as a unity rally between the political sides.

In America, political violence also played out in recent memory from the mid-2010s. But even before then, social unrest and frustration had been building from perceived injustices that made national news. Some of the cases include names like Trayvon Martin, Mike Brown, Heather Heyer, Sandra Bland and more. This series of national news stories led to the creation of *See*

America In Color (SAIC), a social-edge campaign/platform for having a better picture of civic/social issues for a higher level of citizenship. Furthermore, SAIC's 'Operation Mojo' initiative is about advancing a similar unifying message as 'One Love', by how we make our journeys one.

Well, picking up on early American history during John Adams' presidential term, one of his first orders of business was signing into law the Alien and Sedition Acts of 1798. That legislation included four acts, which came from a dislike for those who sided with the French (this was during the period of the French Revolution), and a dislike for how certain media would describe policies of his Administration. The acts allowed for the round-up of some immigrants to be sent back to their countries, as well as the sanctioning of certain media outlets. It might be said that this was the first time in the nation's history that grievance was used as a wedge issue to create chaos as opposed to an edge issue to create progress, like seen in the Declaration of Independence.

Fast forward a few decades when we moved into the presidency of Andrew Jackson. He's best known for signing into law the Indian Removal Act of 1830. This led to the forced migration of five Native American tribes from their land in the east to points west between 1830 and 1850. This period is often called the 'Trail of Tears' and is considered among America's darkest period in forced migration. It might be said that this was a defining time when hate was used as a wedge issue to create chaos as opposed to deploying love as an edge issue to foster connection.

Again, fast forward a few decades and we moved into the presidency of James Buchanan in 1857. He was known to have meddled in the operations of the Supremes Court, which shifted the balance of support against blacks having their freedom. This was during the time of the Dred Scott case, where Scott was seeking his freedom from slavery on the basis that if you're able to escape to a free state, then from that point forward you'd be considered free.

Scott traveled to a free state and stayed temporarily. He then returned to the previous slave state hoping to be free. It was that turn of events which led to the case going all the way up to the Supreme Court. The general sense was that Buchanan had influenced one of the justices on the court to switch his vote, thereby making the Court rule against Scott on his freedom. This debate also led to a speed-up in states seceding from the Union which eventually led to the civil war. It might be said that it was a defining moment not just for starting the civil war, but also for divisiveness being used as a wedge issue to create chaos, as opposed to having diversity as an edge issue to create unity.

What does that mean for more recent events? Well, think of the above history as moments when seeds of grievance, hate and divisiveness were planted in America. Over the past few decades, we've seen those seeds get watered and fertilized in ways like getting shots of 'political steroid'. Furthermore, based on national/world news reports after Barack Obama became the first African American U.S. President, there was racial backslash which gave rise to grievance, hate and divisiveness being used as a wedge issue as opposed to forging a constructive edge issue in political campaigns and on social media platforms.

This further led to misinformation, disinformation and political distrust. This continued to grow all the way through to election certification disputes/disruptions and other forms of social/political division. In addition, there's been growing populist energy in America and other countries that has been a challenge to the world order we've come to know over the last 75-80 years.

America's new 'founding' needs to have a different incentive and fulfillment structure where folks are celebrated for living out their better angels, not their worst instincts. That shouldn't have to wait for the next life but instead be part of the next chapter for our best life. This means not allowing grievance, hate and divisiveness to have a stranglehold on the public square or be rewarded in elections.

It also means preparing future generations not just for having a good job or getting them to vote. But to be engaged so that they're not swayed by politicians who flash money and social pull. This will take living with a renewed sense of civic purpose and commitment to the public good. Along the way we can pass the test of democracy on the way to becoming a more perfect Union.

Chapter 3: The Thought

"Where knowledge is a duty, ignorance is a crime."

What was the initial thought that led Paine to write the book 'Common Sense'? By birth he was an Englishman who decided to emigrate to the United States. Maybe he was intrigued by those who were concerned about the rising tension between Great Britain and its colonies. One would think he'd be among the loyalists who stood on the side of the British. In the end, it might be one or more thought leaders of his time, like Benjamin Franklin, who convinced him to emigrate to the U.S.

The decision to leave your native land to live in an adopted home country isn't something that's happenstance. There's careful thought given to what you'll gain in opportunities and resources as well as what might suffer in family connection and culture. Some people debate whether immigrants have as much claim to the American dream as native-born Americans. At times there's a riff or rub between both sides that gets played up as dislike or distrust. It's why the education you get from SAIC in connecting the dots across history, civics and culture is important. It might even provide more 'smarts' than what you get in the classroom.

America's story is in essence an immigrant story. There were those who left Europe by choice, looking for new ways to build their social cred or biz portfolio. They came for a better life. There's also the other side of the coin for those who were brought here by force from Africa. They weren't given the choice of land and lifestyle but instead sent to work in the fields. That difference in the minds of some people distinguishes blacks in America of African/Caribbean descent, from blacks of African American descent.

One group migrated from their African/Caribbean homeland to the U.S. while the other group are descendants of those who were brought to the U.S. in chains. But from a history standpoint, there really isn't that much 'status difference' between blacks of African/Caribbean descent and those of African American lineage. Both groups are a few generations removed from their fore-parents who were sent to a foreign land as human cargo.

When you consider those who helped set the stage in America's early days, they can be seen in two groups: founding influencers (e.g. Thomas Paine,

Paul Revere) and founding fathers (e.g. George Washington, Alexander Hamilton). Founding Influencers were like the wake-up call brigade, getting others to see the moment required a shift in consciousness as Paine did with his book and Revere did with bell ringing. Founding fathers were like architects who helped build on the backstory of seizing the moment.

Furthermore, there was a small subset who weren't born in the colonies and as such were immigrants, e.g. Paine from England and Hamilton from the island of Nevis in the Caribbean. Their stories have been big inspiration with SAIC and this book, serving as a reminder that whether you're immigrant or native born, there's a role in having America continue to be land of the free, home of the diverse many. Plus, what Paine and Hamilton did to document America's unfolding story through writing is the essence of their legacy.

Hamilton became one of America's founding fathers, serving as an aide to George Washington during the revolution. His service included writing lots of correspondences to other public servants. He's best known these days from the stage play written by Lin-Manuel Miranda. He also authored most of the articles in the Federalist Papers. The Federalist Papers are like the recording notes from the Constitutional Convention which were important with convincing the colonies to sign on to being part of the United States. Hamilton later became the nation's first U.S. Treasury Secretary. Paine and Hamilton are great reminders that the immigrant story runs through the American experience.

For Americans of African descent, it's a bit tricky in tracing their roots since family separation was a painful part of slavery. Family members would be sold as commodities at slave auctions to the highest bidder. Some would be used a 'slave trade sweeteners' in deals that had children taken from their parents. There is a little appreciated aspect of the African American experience that sometimes gets lost in the shuffle. It's the experience of a black child growing up being bombarded with events of injustice and inequality. By the time they're of age, that could have a negative effect. It's important that society doesn't allow that to take the wind out of their sails.

Meanwhile, Americans of European descent might find it easier to trace their roots back to the early days, more so than African Americans. For the former, there's family ancestral history and passed-down stories to help with placing themselves in the journey of America. For the latter, that info is much harder to come by, which makes legacy harder to leverage. Why share all that here? Why go through this preamble of 'life in America 101'? Well, it's another clue behind what Paine once said, "Where knowledge is a duty, ignorance is a crime."

As an immigrant from the Caribbean, in a sense that was sometimes the dilemma. We're raised with the idea that education is the passport to bigger and better things in life. This was stressed throughout our childhood, even at key family moments. For example, my immigrant story was strongly influenced by a family meeting called by my dad. He worked for many years as a civil servant in the government's housing and agriculture sectors. Over that period, he'd worked in various roles, no matter what political party won the last election. This was an important lesson for us on how to be of service to country, not merely by party. At the height of his career, he told us the story of being the odds-on favorite for a promotion.

A certain requirement came with the promotion that he didn't have. His formal education had taken him as far as technical school where he later became a land surveyor by trade. Although he had the know-how and experience for the new job, he didn't get the promotion. That disappointment was the inspiration behind him asking all of us his children to consider taking our education as far as possible. It felt like a crime to see dad get overlooked for the promotion. That was in-part the opening for my immigrant story as well as advancing my education.

That lesson was influential too with creating SAIC. A series of national news stories had left a bad taste, and my ignorance on the issues felt like a crime. This led to a deep dive in American history, the 'Black to America' story and #HometownStrong comebacks. SAIC builds on a framework that's best understood by the shift that occurred back in the day, in going from black & white tv to color tv. The difference in black & white versus color technology is a defining feature in how SAIC brings "smart civics, better picture".

A black & white tv works by beaming a stream of light and varying the intensity of that light to give different shades of black, white and gray. A color tv however, instead of beaming a stream of 'white light', it beams three streams of colored light, red, green and blue. Those who're into visual arts know the term RGB, which is the shortening for those three light streams. So, the aha moment happened in realizing that the deep dive was combining three streams of 'colored light', American history, the 'Black to America' story and #HometownStrong comebacks. This gave a better picture of civic/social issues for a higher level of citizenship.

An often-asked question in media or hometown circles is, "how should Americans feel about certain history lessons being dropped from public policy, textbooks or education curriculums?" Well, the SAIC framework provides some food for thought. If one of the three RGB colors was dropped from the inner workings of the color tv, then the picture on the screen would be affected. The beautiful picture would be lost. Similarly, on eliminating any of those 'history streams' the picture of America will be affected for the worst.

When thought of in another way, if the only light stream used in the color tv is red, without having green and blue, the picture will be hard to watch and enjoy. Similarly, for those who seem to only want to beam the 'white light stream' from America's journey, how's that supposed to be a beautiful picture for telling the story?

Remember from the Star Trek franchise there's the phrase 'Beam me up Scotty"? It was a term used to get back on the spacecraft. The 'transporter' technology would 'beam' someone from one location back to another, usually Starship Enterprise. What SAIC does as a social-edge technology is help transport our understanding from one world to another, from a world of misinformation or disinformation to a world of 'public good sense'. From an outer world of deception to the real world of what's overlooked or underappreciated.

Click Note: *Thomas Paine and Alexander Hamilton are great reminders that the immigrant story runs through the American experience. But when the contribution of other players/groups is overlooked, disregarded or disparaged, then we get a bad picture of America that's hard to enjoy.*

The #HometownStrong 'light stream' also needs some explaining. While doing the deep dive, the information was reviewed with two basic questions in mind: How did 'they' overcome the struggle to get their breakthrough? How did 'they' build excellence to live their best life? The 'they' refers to different racial/ethnic groups that have been challenged by America's moments of grievance, hate and divisiveness. From Native Americans during settlement having their towns and livelihoods destroyed, to African Americans through slavery, to Chinese Americans during the Exclusion Act, to women's right, the 'pride' movement and other suffrage protests, there are shared lessons.

So, with SAIC you'll have a better handle of hot-button issues by how you see America in color, not just in black & white. You'll be equipped with knowledge of history, civics and culture and in the process have a better picture for a higher level of citizenship. Maybe Paine would be proud to see 'Common Sense' have an influence on 'Public Good Sense'. Maybe Hamilton would be impressed by how this book flows from years of writing about SAIC's founding, the way he wrote about America's founding. Maybe the freedom fighters of years past and gamechangers in modern technology would see that with the SAIC model you get more clarity in roots & culture, along with 'smart civic engagement' and social empowerment.

Chapter 4: The Template

"A republic is naturally opposed to the word monarchy, since monarchy is arbitrary power."

In November 1967, Dr. King was invited to speak to students at a Philadelphia school. Earlier that year he released a book entitled, "Where Do We Go from Here: Chaos or Community? He traveled to Jamaica at the beginning of that year to spend time finishing the book. This was a moment of assessing results from the civil rights movement, as well as considering a path forward. By this point the movement was instrumental in securing legislation like the Civil Right Act of 1964 and the Voting Rights Act of 1965. The last of the trifecta was to come in the Housing Act of 1968.

His talk to students centered around another question, "What's in your life's blueprint?" The speech referenced a building's blueprint which shows the features and functions before construction, based on its intended use. He wanted them to focus on having results that add value to their lives on a personal level as was seen with the movement's results on a 'public good sense' level. The key takeaway was found in four points that students needed to nail down as a blueprint to their career and life's work:

- **Belief** in your dignity, worth, somebody-ness; choose self-acceptance over social stigma.

- **Excellence** in whatever you do. Do your best, strive for your best life experience.

- **Act** as if God called you to do it at that moment. Know your strengths and hidden assets.

- **STand** on timeless principles of beauty, love, justice; embrace the struggle for a better life and better America.

It's as if Dr. King was sharing tips for being a BEAST (in a good way) for living their best life. That's how he described building on life's blueprint which relates to who we are in mind, body and core. Based on how God made us for an intended 'use', we're designed with certain features (gifts & talents) and functions (skills & abilities). Those parts of who we are tie-in with human traits that have been around through human history but gained new levels of understanding and appeal over the centuries.

These days what we understand as mind, body and core (spirit) in our human existence is nurtured by how we live-out our calling, purpose and passion. A calling is how we express our higher self, maybe even our better angels where God looks good. For some that's seen in religious or public service pursuits. Your purpose is to serve some earthly good, while passion is how you 'do your thing' in ways that others might say "wow, she's good!" These three hidden assets comprise the blueprint of who we are as humans to maximize fulfillment. Based on God's intended 'use' of our features and functions, they put us on track to do as Dr. King prescribed, which is act as if God called us to the assignment. More on how we lock-in and clock-in with that to 'turn up' in roots & culture coming in a later chapter.

As mentioned before, my dad was a surveyor by training which prepared him to read and interpret a building's blueprint. As a child when a couple rooms were being added to our house, he showed the blueprint to help us with a 'before & after' sense for the pending construction. We got to know what the intended use of those new rooms would be. Seeing it on paper before having the chance to live it and live in it was like what Dr. King was trying to share with students in his talk. The combination of that message with what the founders did in America's startup, speaks to life's blueprint and America's footprint.

How did the founders approach things in defining the new nation? Well, before the Declaration of Independence was written, there were those who organized as the Committee of Correspondence across the colonies. This group of civic-minded local leaders operated around the ideals that would soon define America. They shared updates and strategies for breaking out a shift in consciousness as a nation. Some of the individuals were Samuel Adams, John Hancock and Dr. Joseph Warren, with Adams being among the founding fathers who signed the Declaration of Independence.

Then, during the first 20 years, there were key documents that served as a blueprint/template for building the nation from the ground up. The Declaration of Independence set the stage for the people coming together under a new banner. Beyond the Federalist Papers mentioned previously, there was also the Constitution written in 1787 which took some inspiration from the Magna Carta, a document that was central to establishing a new public format for more enlightened living. The Constitution defined us as a nation and became the law of the land.

Following that was the Bill of Rights, seen as a compromise document between the Federalists and Anti-Federalist wings of political ideology. That's because there was concern about individual rights being trampled on from having a federal (central) government. These documents collectively helped to shape America as a constitutional democratic republic form of government. The 'perfecting of the Union' which includes the 27 Constitutional Amendments, is meant to serve as a democratic process where 'we the people' get to participate in shaping the country by having our voices heard. The republic means electing those who serve as representatives on behalf of 'we the people'.

This template is also supported by what's called 'checks & balances' for how the three branches of government are meant to co-exist in shared responsibility and accountability. The Legislative Branch is the Congress that makes the laws and handles the distribution of funds; the Executive Branch is the Office of the Presidency which sets the vision and governing approach; and the Judicial Branch is the Supreme Court which affirms the laws.

Moreover, what's often overlooked in the rollout of this structure is that the founders often led with a statement of civics before a message or actions in politics. In short, civics means how you represent as elected official, citizen and community member to make 'public good' matter. This also means being aware of the rights, privileges and responsibilities of civic duty. Meanwhile, politics is a means to an end for government programs and policies.

Click Note: *Your life's blueprint relates to who you are in mind, body and core. America's footprint relates to actions that align with the ideals and founding principles that were put in motion for the foundation of the nation's beliefs, people and human spirit.*

The first part of the Declaration of Independence says, "We hold these truths to be self-evident that all men are created equal." The first part of the Constitution says, "We the people in order to form a more perfect Union." Both are examples of leading with civics before politics. One way to hold our public officials accountable is watching whether they're leading with civics or politics. That will give us a sense of how they'll lead with or impart public good sense versus pushing grievance, hate and divisiveness. What they lead with is a preview of how they'll govern. However, there's no guarantee how they campaign will be how they govern, since their politics can also be driven by factors of arbitrary power.

An important reason for America's founding was to go from monarchy-rule (arbitrary power) to self-rule ('we the people' power). We were designed to function as a democratic republic in a representative form of government, not as an autocracy in one-person rule. That template has stood the test of time as people stepped up to serve with a sense of purpose for America's best days. However, things become a challenge from time to time when people enter public service not with a sense of calling and civic duty, but a sense of entitlement and disconnect from the nation's ideals. It might also become a challenge when the rule of the wealth-class gains a stranglehold on the middle/working class or when those who run for office are there simply to serve themselves.

Table

4.1

	Community 1.0	Community 2.0	Community 3.0 and beyond
Phase	**Settlement, Slavery, Independence, Civil War**	**Reconstruction, Segregation, Civil Rights**	Civil rights thru current
Greater Promise	"We hold these truths.."	Emancipation	Post-racial society
Power Struggle	Abolition (freedom)	Segregation (rights)	Disinformation (facts/truth)
What's at stake?	Liberty & Justice	Equality & Opportunity	Fairness/equity, democracy, soul of the nation

In terms of SAIC, there's also a template too. The deep dive led to a blueprint for a better understanding of American history, the 'Black to America' story and #HometownStrong comebacks. This is based on 400+ years of history, civics and culture as the United States of America. As Table 4.1 shows, America's journey has gone through the phases of Settlement, Slavery, Independence, Civil War, Reconstruction, Segregation and Civil Rights.

The struggle has evolved over the years since our nation's founding and has basically been about 'people versus powers.' During the period of 'Community 1.0' the struggle was over abolishing slavery. During 'Community 2.0' the struggle was over ending segregation. Then came 'Community 3.0' with the struggle around fairness and equity. In more recent times the struggle has been about securing democracy and the soul of the nation. As the current times unfold, Community 4.0' might be what *See America In Color* as a template helps affect in the next chapter.

No matter the generation you were born into, charting the way forward based on America's footprint will mean coming together under a new banner in what's being called the Declaration of Emergence. Some people will focus on ways to organize and engage while others will focus on how to educate and empower as 'civic strong' leaders and impact players. Having a deeper sense for American history, the 'black to America' story and #hometownStrong comebacks will help with a shift in consciousness as a nation.

Chapter 5: The Times

"Arguing with a person who has renounced the use of reason is like administering medicine to the dead."

"These days, the times sure are a changing!" Those words might apply to different times of the past 250 years of America's story. Over those centuries we've seen changes occur across social, political and economic areas of life. Moreover, we've seen differences in how folks engaged with the issues of the time, even in more recent periods of Gen X, Millennials and Gen Z.

During the days of the early settlers, much of life's activities involved working the land. This period, often called the Agrarian Age, was built around farming and tending to livestock. It's no accident that some of the early institutions in education have the words 'A&M – Agricultural & Mechanical' in their names. A dominant theme coming out of that early period was the battle over slavery as an enterprise for expanding free-labor markets and benefits.

Then there was the shift to the Industrial Age, to help improve process efficiency and production capability. As cotton became king, merchants needed new ways to go from farm to port to merchandise. This re-engineering of manufacturing eventually spread to other sectors which created opportunities for advancement. A dominant theme from that period was the persistent problem of discrimination that had some feeling sidelined, left out or underrepresented.

From an economic standpoint, we've also evolved in how we make a living. It's no longer limited to what happens on a farm but went from 'hands & feet' to 'blue collar' to 'white collar' to 'gig workers' more recently. What we might think of as a job has also gone through periods of 'refresh' in our lifetimes. A job first starts out in our younger days to make money. It's a way to survive by paying bills and buying necessities. Being able to survive left some holding the bag and others not having any bag. So, to give oneself a leg up, it meant upgrading your skills to thrive by developing a career. While a job is driven by money, a career is driven by money and advancement.

We've all seen those stories of people living their dreams. That somewhat encompasses a career and vocation. This is where your life's work is driven by meaning. You're not just making a living but also living your making and living to the fullest. Whether viewed as a job, career or vocation, your life's journey isn't always found in a single job or a straight-line path, especially since the arrival of the Technology Age and how that continues to affect the job market.

This is where consumer goods and the workplace are influenced or enhanced by the introduction of tech tools and smart features. One of the early examples was the arrival of the color TV set, which helped us to see America in color, not just black & white. This happened during the time of the civil right movement as the color tv helped us see what was happening in the streets around civil disobedience and social unrest, in a more up-close and personal way. That observation was the genesis of SAIC as a concept because color tv helped us see America in color.

Beyond that, we've watched the fast-paced impact of the Information Age with social media playing a major role. While there're positive aspects of technology and access to information, a challenge continues to be that our 'social smarts' hasn't kept pace with our 'tech smarts.' We seem to be able to do more in advancing consumer technology but struggle in advancing public good sense. This fosters the ongoing dilemma seen in the public square where people become frustrated, confused and disillusioned by the social climate.

Flashback to previous years as some folks are old enough to remember when personal computers first hit the marketplace. They functioned on what was called the 'Disk Operating System (DOS).' The user had to remember type-written commands to have the computer perform certain actions. This became cumbersome and time-consuming. As some consumers lost interest and others complained, the tech designers went back to the drawing board and came up with a new & improved operating system, aka 'Windows'. This was a more user-friendly interface to the computer and helped spread greater acceptance for the device as a production-enhancing tool.

There're those in more recent times who're young enough to remember when cell phones first hit the scene as a consumer product. A next-level feature of the device was being able to send instant messages to others, like a faster way of sending morse codes. Things were a bit awkward though, as typing the message often involved multiple taps on a number just to get a single character. This became time-consuming and cumbersome, which challenged tech designers to create a new & improved version, aka the smart phone, which runs on the Apple IOS or Android operating system concept, with the devices having a more user-friendly messaging interface.

Taking those examples and applying to civic/social issues led to creating SAIC as a social-edge campaign & platform. As the deep dive in American history, the 'black to America' story and #HometownStrong comebacks unfolded, there was the sense of resident/citizen frustration and disillusionment with the issues repeating themselves generation after generation. Some of the frustration came from not knowing and for others it came because some were not willing to grow and change. If we can appreciate how technology in consumer devices continues to improve over time, then maybe we can buy-in to a platform that's designed to help us do the same with civic/social issues.

Furthermore, the ongoing improvement in tech creates opportunities in 'smart' systems. From color TVs we now have 'smart TVs' to watch programming via broadcast or streaming. We can connect/mirror an external device to the TV with even more smart features. In my previous career as a computer engineer, we saw that happen in the development process and product line. The work involved large software systems which first introduced the concept of 'Apps'. Remember when you could make a phone call by charging the cost to a calling card? That was made possible by an app on the system that was running in the telephone network. It's also an app that makes it possible for toll-free numbers to be routed to one or more user-specified phone lines, based on region or time-of-day. That's 'smart tech' for user-friendly consumer products.

What we see in tech from then to now can be a model for how we advance in the social arena. When the founders began forming the nation they emphasized the importance of self-evident truths. That was a ground rule for the American experiment and it's also a key aspect of having 'smarts' in technology. In simple terms, software systems that run digital equipment operate off the premise of true or false, represented as 1 or 0.

That's a basic part of how computers work, communicate and interconnect. When that 'truth' becomes compromised or unresolved the computer either ends up in a loop or hits a 'dead end', often known as a critical error. That's some of what we see in the social climate when truth becomes compromised, misplaced or turned into miss-truths. The social/political system gets in a destructive loop or leaves folks stuck in a dead spot as a critical error.

Throughout American history we've seen truth be compromised by how information got communicated. Self-evident truth, like mentioned in the Declaration of Independence that "all men are created equal", includes those obvious facts that are hard to argue with, e.g. the sun is always shining even when it's not visible or the temperature isn't hot. Another example of self-evident truth says human life is meant to be more elevated than animal life as humans have higher consciousness. The problem arises when information gets communicated as 'social truth'. It's like a conversation between friends at a bar after a few drinks. Some things said might sound good, but is it half-truths mixed in with tipsy small talk to become 'social truths'?

Click Note: *We've seen those stories of people living their dreams or rising to higher office who miss the mark on social issues. It takes a new & improved platform that's citizen-friendly for having a better handle on hot-button issues.*

SAIC as a platform offers a unique approach for dealing with the issues of our time through programs in 'smart civic engagement', social empowerment and public good sense. In addition, through collaborations and partnerships, like an app running on a platform, it allows for 'new & improved' advancements along civic & social lines. Furthermore, there's the factor of Artificial Intelligence (AI) as a continuation of that tech/info evolution and revolution. There're options to synthesize, monetize and energize the interface with issues and innovations in the rapid pace of our times.

With SAIC functioning like a 'Hometown IOS' platform, we can unpack the issues based on a 'social operating system' mindset. As our experience with the tech model grows through use of the device and the supporting interface, the more comfortable using it becomes. Similarly, the more SAIC helps others connect the dots across history, civics and culture, the more value its use and the and chance for impact it offers. Not to be overlooked, the 'AI' in SAIC brings 'automatic intelligence' through the framework and supporting interface, for having a better handle of hot-button issues by how we see America in color, not just in black & white.

The overall benefit is reducing the frustration we feel around certain news reports. We can be better informed on the issues and not be unduly influenced by grievance, hate and divisiveness. We can minimize getting into heated debates since arguing with a person who has renounced truth or the use of reason is like administering medicine to the dead. Let the 'dead' be consumed by the ignorance and implications of the times that's likely to bury the dead.

SAIC helps free up energy to focus on life, liberty and the pursuit of happiness. In the long run, what you do to make a living is just part of the story. Who you are in mind, body and core as well as how you are of service to the marketplace and mankind is the real story for making a difference. The reward is the paycheck you get from your talents and abilities and the fulfillment you have from living your best life.

Chapter 6: The Turn-up

"Experience has shown even under the best forms of government, those entrusted with power have, in time, by slow operations, perverted it into tyranny."

As the sun rose on those October mornings after the last Revolution battle at Yorktown, news spread that General Charles Cornwallis from the British forces had surrendered to George Washington and the patriot forces. A few months later, the British parliament passed a resolution calling for the end of the war. This might have been the end of the revolution chapter of the story but was also a turning point in America's founding as a nation.

The first 20 years of America's dawning included a sequence of events with an orchestrated rollout in purpose, plans and promise. We might think of this period as defining The People's Plan, which began in the formation phase of letting go of old habits/dependencies and creating a new charter for governing. The initial framework in the Articles of Confederation established some principles and practices for moving from colonies to States, from British subjects to American citizens. These foundational steps symbolize America's early footprint.

Working together as a new co-operative had its challenges and security gaps. There was even concern about who's really in-charge when it came to carrying out certain aspects of the charter or responding to external threats. This unsettling period meant having to go from turning point to another round of debates and decisions. The grand meet-up at the Constitutional Convention in Philadelphia resulted in a new organizing structure for governance and shared guarantees.

The remaining time in the first 20 years continued with the education of 'we the people' across the colonies on the readout from the Constitutional Convention. It also involved creating or building institutions for more formal learning. Many of the colleges we know today as 'Ivy League' schools, are among America's oldest venues of higher learning. Maybe over time, that's one reason for being considered as 'special' institutions since there's so much history rooted in their existence.

As things moved along, the nation wanted to emphasize the 'united' part of its name. This was captured in a motto based on the Latin phrase E

Pluribus Unum, which means 'Out of Many, One!' It was an instrumental time where we saw efforts to empower or 'turn up' among the people and nation. As a side note, there's close similarity between America's motto and that of Jamaica. In the case of Jamaica, the motto says, 'Out of Many, One People'.

Click Note: *How we 'turn-up' big in our skillset and life's work across family, community and country is shaped by having a new vibe in look & feel, swag in style & substance, with more hustle & flow in the bag.*

Fast forward to a later period and there's another point in America's journey that might also be seen as a turning point, which later inspired a 'turn up' across the nation. In 1954, the Supreme Court issued the Brown vs Board of Education decision that declared segregation unlawful. This ruling had major implications for how States began slowly opening the door to equality in education and access to opportunity.

Then, a sequence of events followed, among them the killing of Emmett Till in 1955 and Rosa Park's refusal to give up her seat in the front of the bus later that year in Montgomery Alabama. This led to a new phase 'turn up' in the civil rights movement. By 1958, Dr. King released a book called 'Stride Toward Freedom: The Montgomery Story' that recapped those moments and helped set the stage for a young people 'turn up' in the movement. His book served as inspiration to many, including two students at North Carolina A&T University, who along John Lewis, were among the founders of the Student Nonviolent Coordinating Committee, better known as SNCC.

In American history we have Thomas Paine whose book 'Common Sense' made the case for the Declaration of Independence and the nation's founding. We also have Dr. King, from the 'Black to America' story, whose book 'Stride Toward Freedom' made the case for change through civil rights. Paine wasn't the only one involved with how 'The People's Plan' unfolded. Other voices helped forge a new beginning. Similarly, King wasn't the only one advocating for change and 'The Turn-up Agenda' back in his day. In both cases they were able to rally people 'out of many as one' to the cause of the moment.

What if we combined the legacies of Thomas Paine and Dr. King in a new way? Paine's work inspired the Declaration of Independence while King's work inspired a 'turn up' in America. Well, that might cause us to rally around the Declaration of Emergence as follows:

"We hold these truths to be self-evident that all men are created equal, that they are endowed by their Creator with certain unalienable rights, civic virtues and hidden assets, among them in mind, body and core to live their best life."

These words represent the ultimate 'tun up' in life's blueprint and America's footprint. Throughout history folks have had to 'turn up' by how they overcame the struggle to get their breakthrough. We've seen this in various suffrage movements that challenged America to live up to its ideals and live out its truths. One way to understand overcoming the struggle is where truth is seen as 'the real u that hopes.' It's the truth that sets you free, that helps you live your authentic self. But there're others who seem to live their truth as 'the real u that hurts' by how they bring cruelty and pain to people and situations. The truth that America has always needed is what will set the nation free.

How folks 'turn up', not just to overcome struggle but also to build excellence means operating with life's blueprint in 'BEAST' mode as mentioned previously. That blueprint includes your hidden assets, described as calling, purpose, passion and dreams. To take them a step further, how you 'turn up' those assets work like directional coordinates in GPS. This technology is great for getting you from start to finish, even with potential delays and detours along the way. GPS works by successfully navigating in directions going east, west, north or south towards your destination.

Similarly, the hidden assets help guide life's journey to points east, west, north or south towards your best life experience. They get you to move in different directions without losing your bearing. If the internal system of a plane's GPS can get you from takeoff to landing, then the hidden assets are just as effective as GPS, God's Positioning System, for takeoff in career and landing in success. You're moving in the direction your life should go.

America's story includes times of turning left or turning right in its thinking. This has played out by electing different political parties and choosing various governing philosophies. It showed up in ways that enhanced or sometimes rattled world order. It has also taken hard-right and hard-left turns that led to turbulent periods in the nation's history. Without having to recall them all here, those periods might have felt like moments of tyranny. This is where governance decisions are often short-sighted, maybe even detrimental to the public good.

Whether life's journey has felt like taking a road trip using GPS or playing a video game using a controller, there's a method to the madness for stabilizing the experiencing, getting to the end and raising the score. With video games, the better you are at overcoming the obstacles, the higher chance there is for unleashing hidden rewards. Those rewards in tools or resources get released when a player achieves excellence in performance. Your next move or America's next chapter of excellence will mean navigating life's journey like GPS, mastering skillset like playing video games and raising the social score towards a more perfect Union.

In the end, how you 'turn up' in roots & culture is like bringing 'DJ energy' to your skillset on the job and life's work in the marketplace, as if skillset and life's work were two turntables. Think about a DJ using two turntables to 'turn up' the energy at a party. In times past a DJ showed up with two or three crates, having a collection of records across decades and genres. Nowadays the music is all digital. The key is to play the right mix of records from different albums to keep the party jumping. As you do the things to 'turn up', it takes mixing life's blueprint and America's footprint like two turntables. It means having the right 'crates' in history, civics and culture to level-up in the workplace and social space.

Chapter 7: The Takeaways

"He whose heart is firm and whose conscience approves his conduct, will pursue his principles [for a lifetime]."

America arriving at its 250th birthday represents a milestone in the annals of time. The celebrations and commemorations offer moments to look back and reflect. As with the deep dive in American history, the 'Black to America' story and #HometownStrong comebacks which led to SAIC, the milestone also allows a chance for charting the course in America's next chapter. What might the new phase look like in the unfolding saga?

The road traveled so far in America's journey involved seven phases: Settlement, Slavery, Independence, Civil War, Reconstruction, Segregation and Civil Rights. The first 20 years laid down America's footprint, otherwise known here as The People's Plan. While Thomas Paine was instrumental in making the case for America's founding and the Declaration of Independence, many others did their part across the colonies as Committees of Correspondence. They were often local leaders committed to the public good.

As years passed, the emerging nation saw turns to the left and to the right in ideology, sometimes sharp turns that tested the souls of men. Along the way there've been periods of struggle and challenges which were addressed by 'The Turn-up Agenda' in those times, through suffrage movements around civic engagement and social change. History reveals that every 60-70 years on average, America has had a wake-up call resulting in a new phase or historical landmark.

Click Note: *The moral of the story here is that over the years it seems America has been developing a tumor that's been growing larger in the social space, affecting our civic mindset.*

The 1954 Supreme Court ruling in Brown vs Board of Education represented one of those moments where the civil rights movement gained new momentum. That phase carried us through to the early part of the new millennium in the 21st century. The historical record might point to the timeframe of 2020 where a new phase began to take shape. In the past, after a period of divisiveness, we entered Reconstruction. So, we have a chance for a new phase going forward.

Then there was the Kerner Commission report in response to the summer 1967 uprisings in some communities. The report noted that we were moving towards two societies, one black one white – separate and unequal. Well, it seems in more recent times that our public discourse is moving towards two worlds: one of life, liberty and happiness, the other of grievance, hate and divisiveness. But we have a chance in the 21ˢᵗ century to emerge into a new phase being called Reconstitution, with America's 250ᵗʰ birthday.

While it isn't necessarily about rewriting the U.S. Constitution, it supports the idea of taking steps in current times that draw on lessons from the past to inject 'smarts' in the future. For example, back in the mid-1800s when political conventions first got off the ground, blacks and other racial groups weren't allowed to attend. This caused those in the black suffrage movement to begin hosting their own conventions where the Constitution would be read, explained and affirmed as something that should mean equality for all. Another example is when a print newspaper or magazine publication would have an anniversary edition where they'd include a 'supplement insert' with that edition. Maybe with America's 250ᵗʰ birthday and next chapter, we might consider a 'Constitution Supplement' to go along with the founding document.

What if that also opens the door to consider a social rebrand in America's public image and policy portfolio? If we're to have the next generation onboard, it might mean having their buy-in on a new mindset around 'American Essentialism', since it appears that American Exceptionalism has lost it way. The term Essentialism basically means doing those things where there's alignment with your core blueprint to best fulfill your assignment. It's in how the blueprint guides our footprint from ideals and essence to existence. Moreover, this would mean that who we are as individuals or a nation would aim to reflect our best yet, not simply who we advertise ourselves to be. Now, if there isn't alignment, then there would need to be a change, whether in process or blueprint (essence) for a better existence. American Essentialism could help move us towards a more perfect Union.

Just remember, the founders were thinking about steps for their present situation as well as for posterity. Therefore, if there's a misalignment with America's ideals, we must shift by how we reset and recommit to a civic imprint in the nation's move to improve. We're at another moment in history that requires a shift in consciousness, maybe even a rewiring of our social impulses. There's a personal story that helps bring that point home.

A few years ago, a swelling appeared on my left thigh. It wasn't clear what was the cause. I decided to keep a watch, thinking it may go away. After a couple years, the swelling got bigger and was causing some pain and discomfort when exercising, climbing stairs or other physical activity. At my next annual physical, my doctor wasn't sure either, so he referred me to the care of an oncology surgeon.

Upon further medical tests, we learned that the tumor was close to a key artery that carries blood up/down my leg. The tumor was also wrapped around two or three nerve fibers, where removing it would require cutting off those nerves and possibly losing the ability to walk. The doctor and his team performed delicate surgery and it's a miracle that I'm still walking, since there was a chance that the nerve fibers being cut might include the one used for movement of the limbs. The doctor thinks that either it wasn't the one responsible for movement, or that the physical impulses needed for movement were already being transferred to other remaining nerve fibers that were free from interference of the tumor being removed. The body might have done a 'rewiring switch' in functions. Thankfully, the tests on the tumor showed no cancerous trace or spread in the body.

The moral of the story here is that America has been developing a tumor that's been growing larger in the social space, affecting our civic mindset. The tumor upon further tests is made up of grievance, hate and divisiveness, which has been growing over the past 20 years. How we remove the tumor will require delicate surgery to avoid damage to other parts of our nation's well-being. We can take notes from Thomas Paine who dealt with a tumor from British rule in America's social space back in his time and made the case for America's founding. We can take comfort in the example of Paul Revere whose actions provide clues for how we organize and engage, educate and empower. This way the body politic or the larger body known as 'we the people' might do the 'rewiring switch' in the social space and civic mindset from the tumor being removed.

Furthermore, think of this Reconstitution phase like what happens when you jumpstart a dead battery. You'll connect cables between a strong battery and a drained battery. Then after a short time the car with the drained battery gets a boost from the car with the strong battery. Well, during this next phase, we can be a more 'civic strong' nation through knowledge transfer of civic/social issues built around The People's Plan. Moreover, just like there's a 'juice transfer' that happens between batteries, The Turn Up Agenda offers a similar juice transfer in 'smart civic engagement.'

One important aspect from America in 1776 and 250 years later points to public good sense. During the first 20 years, the focus of the nation was much about building the apparatus and infrastructure for 'we the people' doing something bigger than oneself. These days much of the energy happens to be spent building the apparatus/infrastructure of running for elections. Once elections are over it seems there's a letdown. There isn't as much a sense for a higher calling, deeper purpose or greater good to be realized as it was in 1776. That's a key reason for efforts behind 'Operation Mojo' to direct focus and energy to something beyond what's required for political campaigns and other machinations.

Along with those 'civic strong' plans, we should find ways to institutionalize efforts where the nation does more in perfecting the Union. We can connect these steps across industry sectors and segments of society into what might be thought of as 'Committees of Civic Ends.' During our founding there was a process of coming together around certain civic virtues for impact and public good, like liberty & justice, rights & responsibilities, goodness & hope. That was in response to people feeling exhausted by British Monarchy rule.

Nowadays there's a need to turn exhaustion/frustration into engagement, grievance into empowerment, especially when you consider that America's founding was influenced by The Enlightenment period. This means that 'we the people' can build on a shift in consciousness as a nation, one community at a time, across educational, social, developmental and fiscal lines. This will sync with the historical model to level-up our nation's focus on education, awareness, consciousness and purpose.

In terms of serving and servicing the marketplace, many industry leaders know about B2B (business to business) and B2C (business to consumer) for having strong earnings/value. Those strategies help open lanes of commerce and streams of income. What's needed in the 21st century for a more perfect Union is the concept of B2CE (business to civic ends). This model will help open lanes of engagement and streams of public good. It will offer a framework on impacting, serving and servicing the civic marketplace for having 'strong citizens.'

That's where the Strong Citizens Association of America (SCAA) will be of value. In a nutshell, the SCAA is to communities/hometowns as the NCAA is to colleges/universities. What helped inspire the SCAA? Well, in November of 1869 the first college football game was played in Central New Jersey between Rutgers University and Princeton University. It's why Central Jersey is often considered the birthplace of college football. Over time, the game became dangerous, brutal and even deadly as folks lost their lives on the field. Some key players back then had concerns and pulled together an effort that led to forming the NCAA to help rein things in.

Well, in recent times our civic space and public discourse have gotten dangerous, brutal, even deadly. We can take a page from those 'public good soldiers' in forging an organization to address current concerns and institutionalize a response. In the process, we can look to make progress along what might be considered as the 'Sovereignty Scale'. It's a way to assess whether we're moving up in the direction of GOAT (greatest of all times) as a nation or moving down in the direction of becoming a GHOST (greatest hell on soil times) of a nation.

It's well known that New York is considered the Financial/Media Capital of the world based on the large number of personnel from those sectors. It's the 'boots on the ground' of people and resources that make things happen. Similarly, California is often seen as the showbiz capital of the world when it comes to celebrity star power in entertainment. Well, we can build on that concept when it comes to being the Civics Capital of the world, by having boots on the ground in people and resources for a higher level of citizenship.

In America's next chapter, we'll need a shift in consciousness as happened in the previous phases of our nation's journey. As we move towards what's being called the Reconstitution phase, we can re-align with our founding principles at this tipping point. This will help us emerge from a state of emergency in governance, with next-level social impact resources and boots on the ground in civic engagement.

Consider for a moment a chef trying to make a more perfect curry chicken, oxtails or some other Caribbean dish. That would require having the right ingredients, utensils and recipe (process) to make it happen. This would also mean gaining experience over time towards being at their 'cooking best.' In this next phase of America's journey of becoming a more perfect Union, it will mean having the right ingredients of vision, conviction and voice, along with a process for being at our 'hometown best.'

What we've tried to do in these pages is offer a gameplan that makes the case for America's next chapter, as well as the Declaration of Emergence for your best life. We've shared examples for connecting the dots across history, civics and culture for the public good and to make good sense. The combination of those tracks we hope presents a framework and inner feel that makes public good sense. America has come a long way since its founding, but there's a new dawning on the horizon that we look forward to impacting for years to come.

Bibliography References & Reading List

1. Blain, Keisha N. (Editor), "Wake up America: Black Women on the Future of Democracy." New York: W. W. Norton & Company, 2024.

2. Brettschneider, Corey, "The Presidents and the People: Five Leaders Who Threatened Democracy and the Citizens Who Fought to Defend It." New York: W. W. Norton & Company, 2024.

3. Bruni, Frank, "The Age of Grievance." New York: Avid Reader Press, 2024.

4. Frost, Amanda, "You are not American: Citizenship Stripping from Dred Scott to the Dreamers." Boston: Beacon Press, 2021.

5. Gadson, Marcus Alexander, "Sedition: How America's Constitutional Order Emerged from Violent Crisis." New York: New York University Press, 2025.

6. Gordon-Reed, Annette, "On Juneteenth." New York: Liveright Publishing Corp., 2021.

7. Glaude, Eddie S., Jr., "Begin Again: James Baldwin's American and Its Urgent Lessons For Our Own." New York: Crown, 2020.

8. Hasak-Lowy, Todd, "We are Power: How Nonviolent Activism Changes the World." New York: Abrams Books, 2020.

9. Healy, Thomas, "Soul City: Race, Equality, and the Lost Dream of an American Utopia." New York: Metropolitan Books, Henry Holt and Company, 2021.

10. Howe, Neil, "The Fourth Turning is Here: What the Seasons of History Tell Us About How and When This Crisis Will End." New York: Simon & Schuster, 2023.

11. Jacobs, A.J., "The Year of Living Constitutionally: One Man's Humble Quest to Follow the Constitution's Original Meaning." New York: Crown, 2024.

12. King, Martin Luther, Jr., "Stride Toward Freedom: The Montgomery Story." New York: Harper & Brothers, Publishers, 1958.

13. King, Martin Luther, Jr., "Where Do We Go From Here: Chaos or Community?" Boston: Beacon Press, 2010.

14. Lalami, Laila, "Conditional Citizens: On Belonging in America." New York: Pantheon Books, 2020.

15. Larson, Edward J., "Franklin & Washington: The Founding Partnership." New York: William Morrow, an imprint of HarperCollins Publishers, 2020.

16. Leonhardt, David, "Ours Was the Shining Future: The Story of the American Dream." New York: Random House, 2023.

17. Lepore, Jill, "We The People: A History of the U.S. Constitution." New York: Liveright Publishing Corporation, 2025.

18. Levin, Yuval, "American Covenant: How the Constitution Unified Our Nation - And Could Again." New York: Basic Books, 2024.

19. Loewen, James W., "Lies My Teacher Told Me: Everything American History Textbooks Get Wrong." New York: New Press, 2019.

20. McCullough, David, "History Matters." New York: Simon & Schuster, 2025.

21. Meacham, Jon, "His Truth is Marching On: John Lewis and the Power of Hope." New York: Random House, 2020.

22. Nichols, Thomas M., "Our Own Worst Enemy: The Assault from Within on Modern Democracy." New York, NY: Oxford University Press, 2021.

23. Nwanevu, Osita, "The Right of the People: Democracy and the Case for a New American Founding." New York: Random House, 2025.

24. Paine, Thomas, "Collected Writings - Common Sense; The Crisis; Rights of Man; The Age of Reason; Agrarian Justice." Rare Treasure Editions, 2024.

25. Putnam, Robert D, "The Upswing: How America Came Together a Century Ago and How We Can Do It Again." New York: Simon & Schuster, 2020.

26. Richardson, Heather Cox, "Democracy Awakening: Notes on the State of America." New York: Viking, 2023.

27. Ricks, Thomas E., "First Principles: What America's Founders Learned from the Greeks and Romans and How That Shaped Our Country." New York: Harper, 2020.

28. Sharpton, Al, "Righteous Troublemakers: Untold Stories of the Social Justice Movement in America." Toronto, Ontario, Canada: Hanover Square Press, 2022.

29. Theoharis, Jeanne, "King of the North: Martin Luther King's Life of Struggle Outside the South." New York: The New Press, 2025.

30. Tucker, Phillip Thomas, "Brothers in Liberty: The Forgotten Story of the Free Black Haitians Who Fought for American Independence." Essex, Connecticut: Stackpole Books, 2023.

31. Weiss, Elaine, "Spell Freedom: The Underground Schools that Built the Civil Rights Movement." New York: One Signal Publishers/Atria, 2025.

About the Author

Douette O. 'Doc' Cunningham is ... a motivator who affirms the notion that "life is meant to be lived with purpose." He has worked with many aspects of technology and human development during his career, which included 10 years of IT experience with the world's largest R&D Consortium.

Doc made the shift from Corporate America to pursue his passion and live his dreams. He's had many opportunities to showcase his abilities, share his philosophies and market his strategies around civics, career, culture and community. His True Calling is geared towards the social-edge campaign/platform to *See America In Color* (SAIC).

Friends/peers say Doc is a great communicator because he **speaks to and through** people. He blends his gift of motivation with his passion for "purpose in living." This special combination makes him a **practitioner and commentator** who takes the daily news and current affairs and turns them into heart-grabbing soundbites.

Acknowledgment

This book came together through years of research in history, civics and culture. It is also made possible by the support of many who, while not sure where my journey was going, were sure that they had my back.

Having the book available to you the consumer involved the professionalism and publishing expertise of the team at Book Publishing Group LLC. They carefully guided the steps needed to have this be another masterful work from their operation. That, along with years of my writing and blogging seems to have helped make things come together seamlessly.

There are many colleagues and friends who've watched the concepts develop over the years. This includes two long-time supporters who assisted with proofreading and defining a social media strategy.

Lastly, if this book gets your attention, it might also be due to the 'Hometown Collective' of like-minded individuals who recognize those moments where unity of purpose can be a defining aspect of community engagement.